Advanced Piano

Weddings
Arranged by ALBERT MENDOZA

The Most Requested Pop Selections Arranged for Wedding Ceremonies

Music is one of the most cherished parts of the wedding ceremony. This collection—featuring favorite and heartwarming selections from contemporary pop artists—can be used for prelude music or for special moments during the service. The famous "Bridal Chorus" (Wagner) and "Wedding March" (Mendelssohn) are also included to give the pianist all of the arrangements necessary for the entire wedding. Approximate performance times, optional repeats, and optional segues are included to further facilitate planning. For continuous music, all of the pop songs can be played back-to-back—by beginning with "This I Promise You" and following the segue directions at the end of each arrangement.

The tender chords in Michael Bublé's "Home," the soaring melody in ★NSYNC's "This I Promise You," the uplifting chorus in Josh Groban's "You Raise Me Up," and all of the other wonderful musical moments are certain to provide the perfect backdrop for any wedding service, as well as many hours of enjoyment for the pianist who wishes to be a *Popular Performer*.

CONTENTS

Bridal Chorus	Richard Wagner	2
Faithfully	Journey	10
Home	Michael Bublé	14
The Prayer	Celine Dion and Andrea Bocelli	5
This I Promise You	★NSYNC	20
Up Where We Belong	*An Officer and a Gentleman*	25
Valentine	Jim Brickman	30
Wedding March	Felix Mendelssohn	34
You Raise Me Up	Josh Groban	36

To Melinda and Scott

Produced by
Alfred Music Publishing Co., Inc.
P.O. Box 10003
Van Nuys, CA 91410-0003
alfred.com

Printed in USA.

No part of this book shall be reproduced, arranged, adapted, recorded, publicly performed, stored in a retrieval system, or transmitted by any means without written permission from the publisher. In order to comply with copyright laws, please apply for such written permission and/or license by contacting the publisher at alfred.com/permissions.

ISBN-10: 0-7390-7512-8
ISBN-13: 978-0-7390-7512-8

Cover Photo: © istockphoto / fabphoto

Bridal Chorus
(from *Lohengrin*)

(Approx. Performance Time – 2:30)

By Richard Wagner
Arr. Albert Mendoza

(Approx. Performance Time – 4:30)

THE PRAYER

Words and Music by Carole Bayer Sager and David Foster
Arr. Albert Mendoza

© 1998 WARNER-TAMERLANE PUBLISHING CORP.
All Rights Reserved

Home

(Approx. Performance Time – 5:15)

Words and Music by
Michael Bublé, Alan Chang and Amy Foster
Arr. Albert Mendoza

© 2005 I'M THE LAST MAN STANDING MUSIC, IHAN ZHAN MUSIC, SONGS OF UNIVERSAL, INC. and ALMOST OCTOBER SONGS
All Rights for I'M THE LAST MAN STANDING MUSIC Administered by WB MUSIC CORP.
All Rights for IHAN ZHAN MUSIC Administered by WARNER-TAMERLANE PUBLISHING CORP.
All Rights Reserved

(Approx. Performance Time – 5:00)

Up Where We Belong
(from *An Officer and a Gentleman*)

Words by Will Jennings
Music by Jack Nitzsche and Buffy Sainte-Marie
Arr. Albert Mendoza

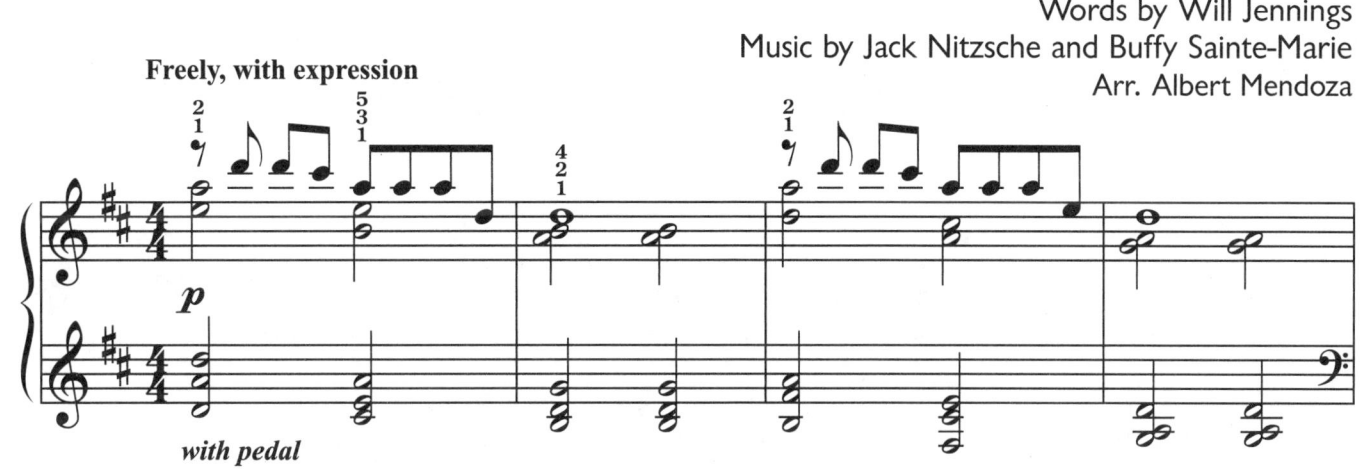

© 1982 ENSIGN MUSIC CORP. and SONY/ATV HARMONY, 8 Music Square West, Nashville, TN 37203
All Rights Reserved

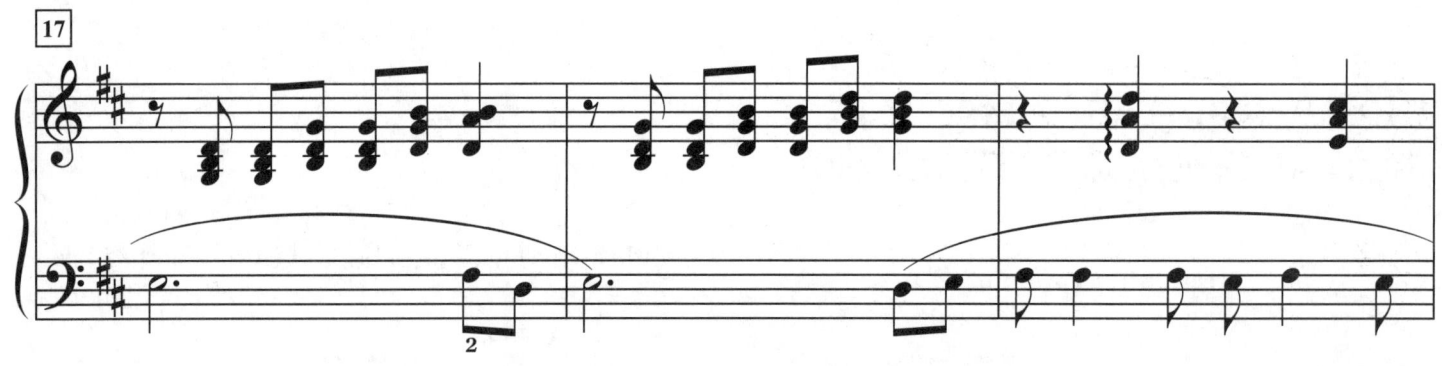

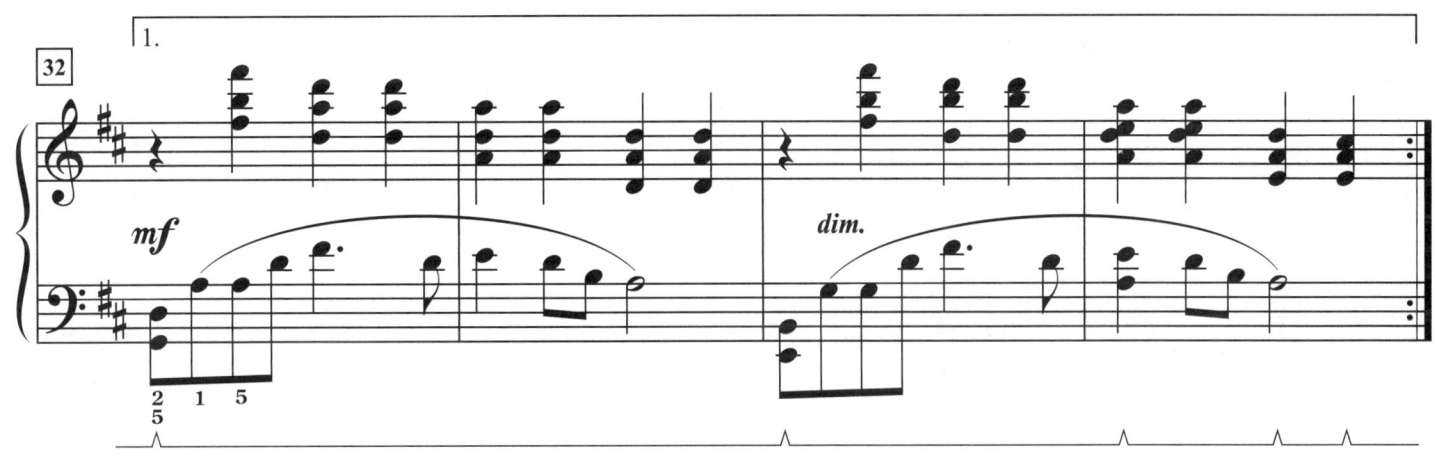

42
4
2
1
poco accel.
simile
molto cresc.
45
5
3
2
Tempo I
rit.
ff
3
1
5
2
48
51

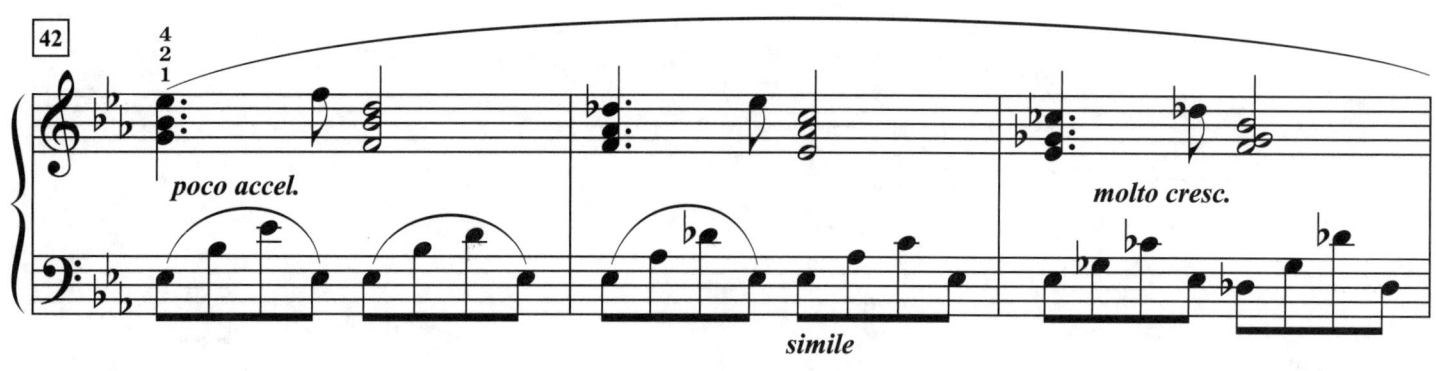

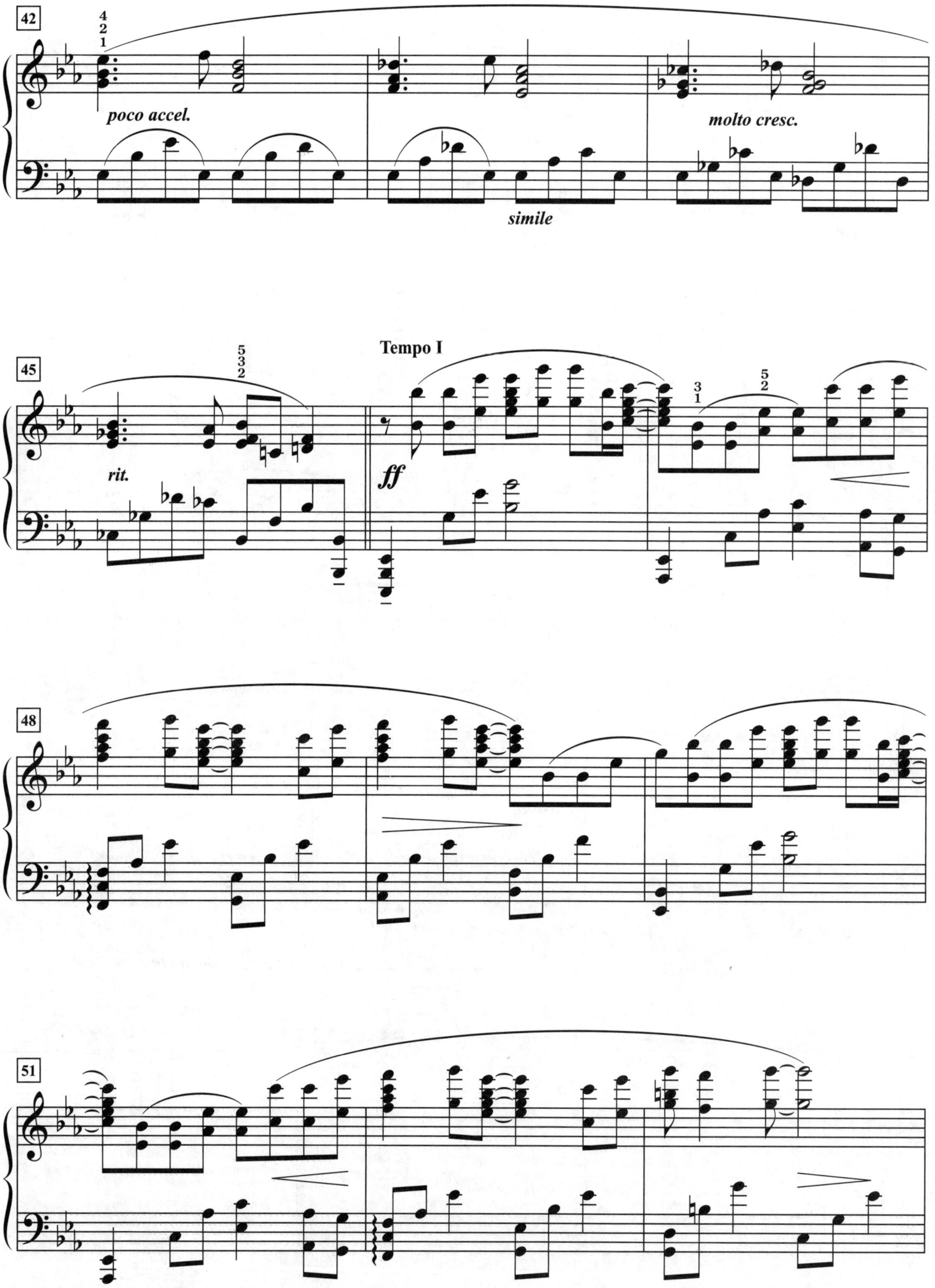

VALENTINE

(Approx. Performance Time – 3:30)

Words and Music by Jim Brickman and Jack Kugell
Arr. Albert Mendoza

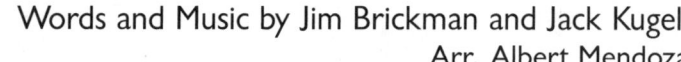

© 1996 BRICKMAN ARRANGEMENT and EMI APRIL MUSIC INC./DOXIE MUSIC
Print Rights for BRICKMAN ARRANGEMENT Administered Worldwide by ALFRED MUSIC PUBLISHING CO., INC.
All Rights Reserved

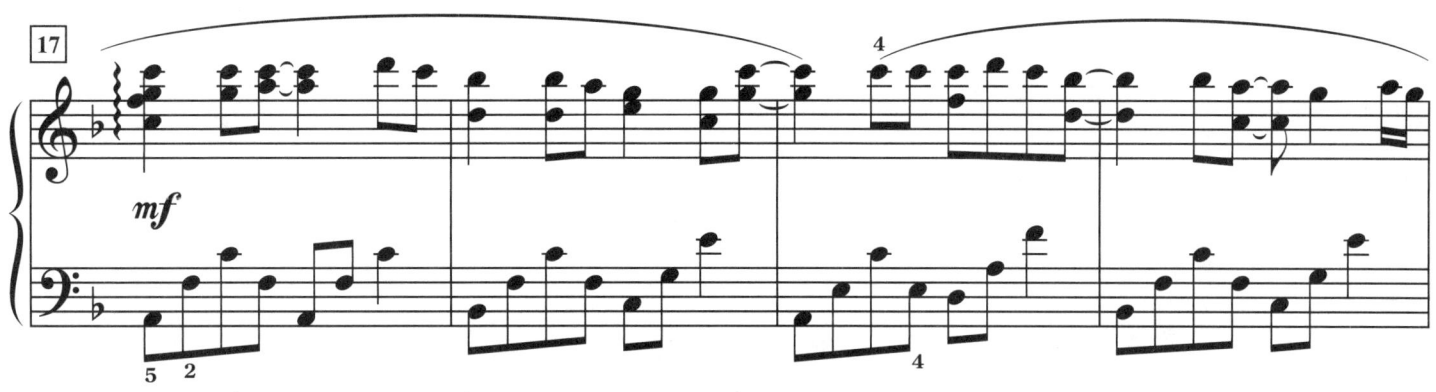

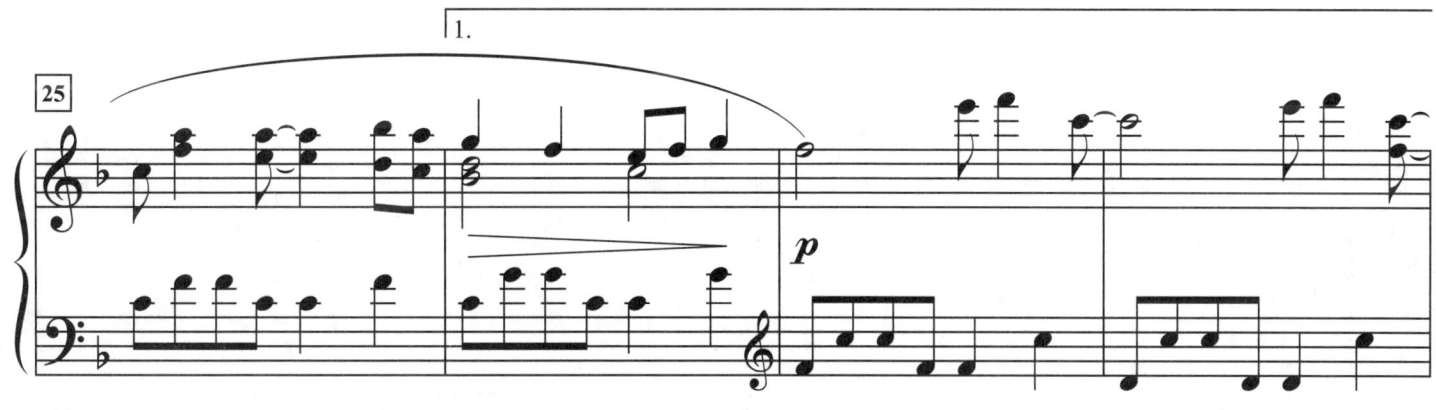

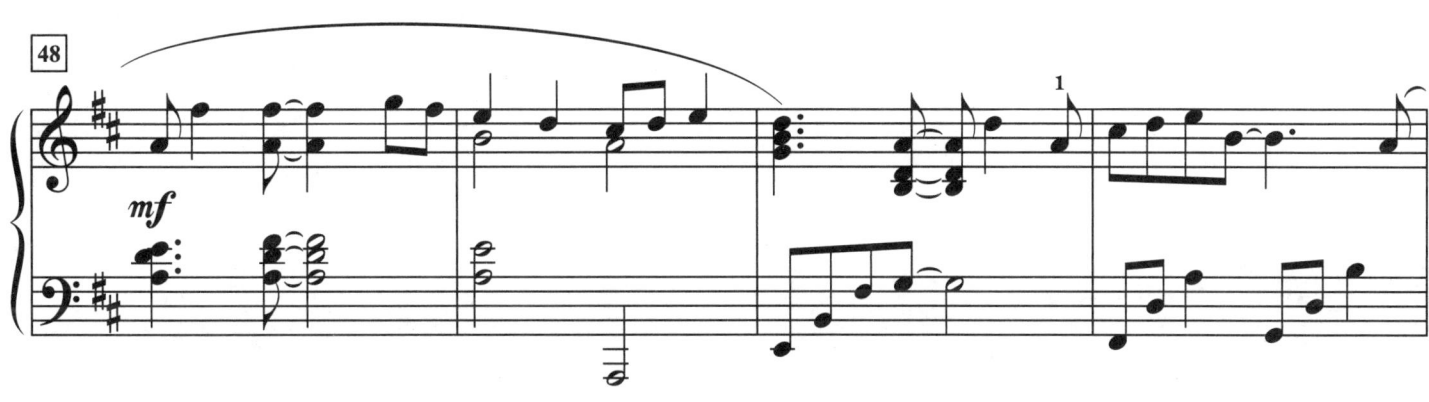
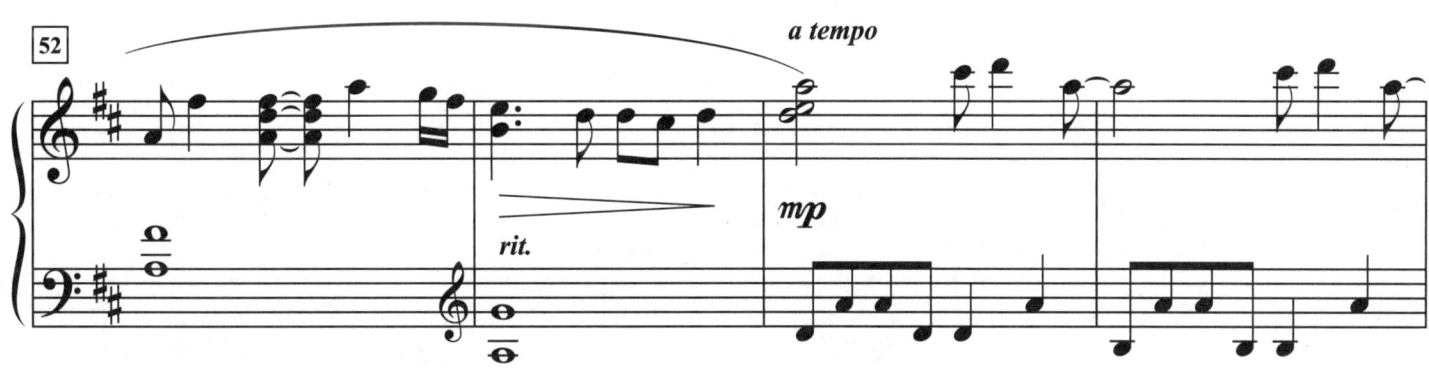

(segue, p. 14)

34

(Approx. Performance Time – 1:30)

Wedding March
(from *A Midsummer Night's Dream*)

By Felix Mendelssohn
Arr. Albert Mendoza

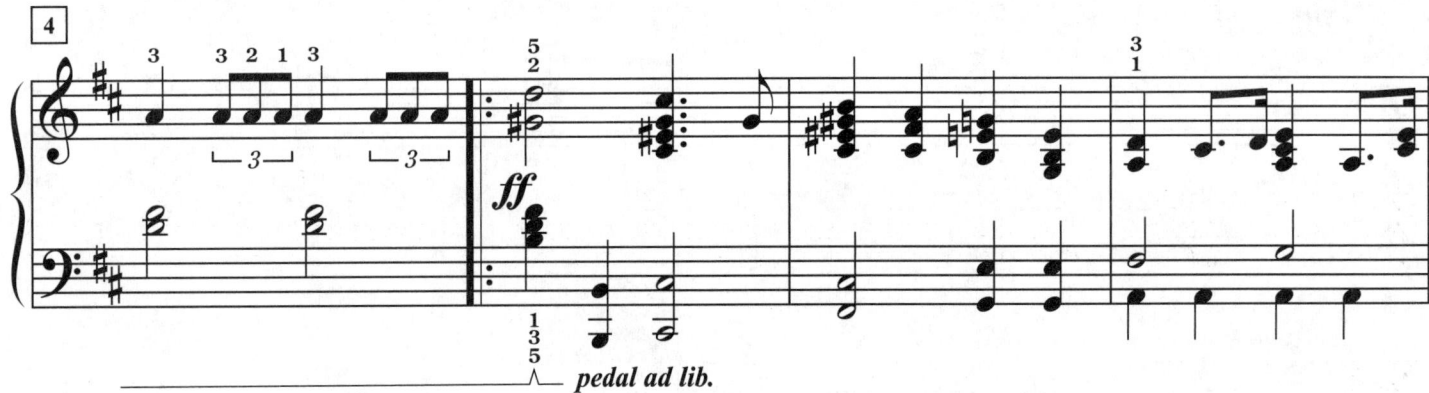

© 2010 ALFRED MUSIC PUBLISHING, INC.
All Rights Reserved

You Raise Me Up

(Approx. Performance Time – 4:30)

Words and Music by Rolf Lovland and Brendan Graham
Arr. Albert Mendoza

© 2002 UNIVERSAL MUSIC PUBLISHING, A Division of UNIVERSAL MUSIC AS and PEERMUSIC (Ireland) LTD.
All Rights for ROLF LOVLAND and UNIVERSAL MUSIC PUBLISHING Administered in the U.S. and Canada by
UNIVERSAL-POLYGRAM INTERNATIONAL PUBLISHING, INC. (Publishing) and ALFRED MUSIC PUBLISHING CO., INC. (Print)
All Rights Reserved

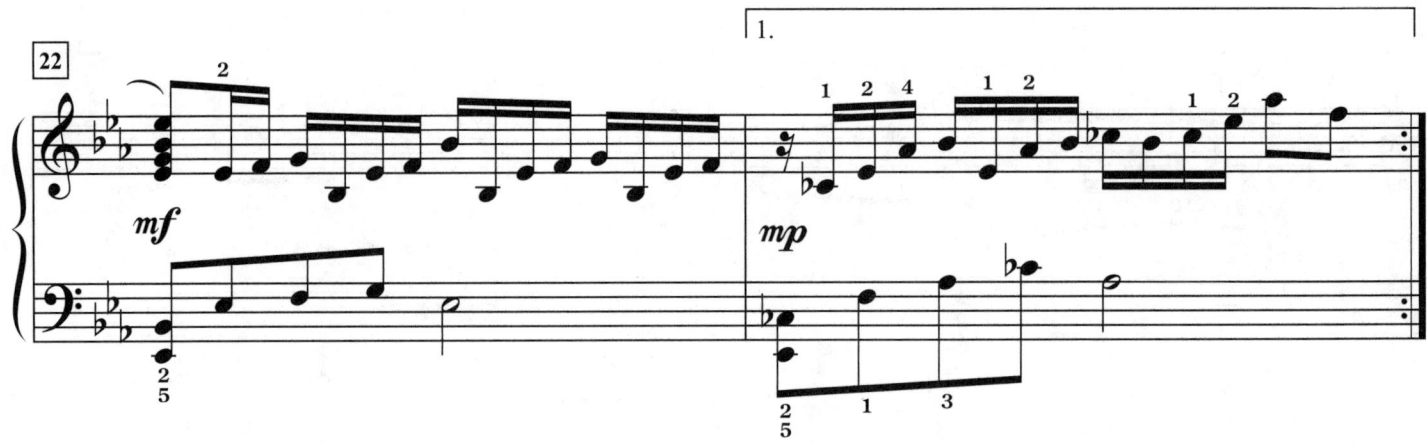

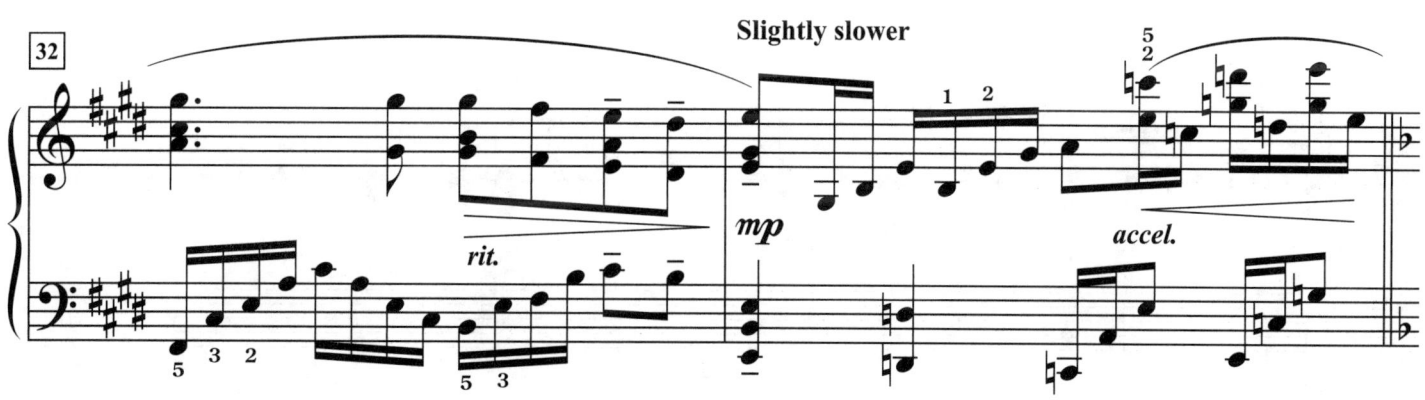

40

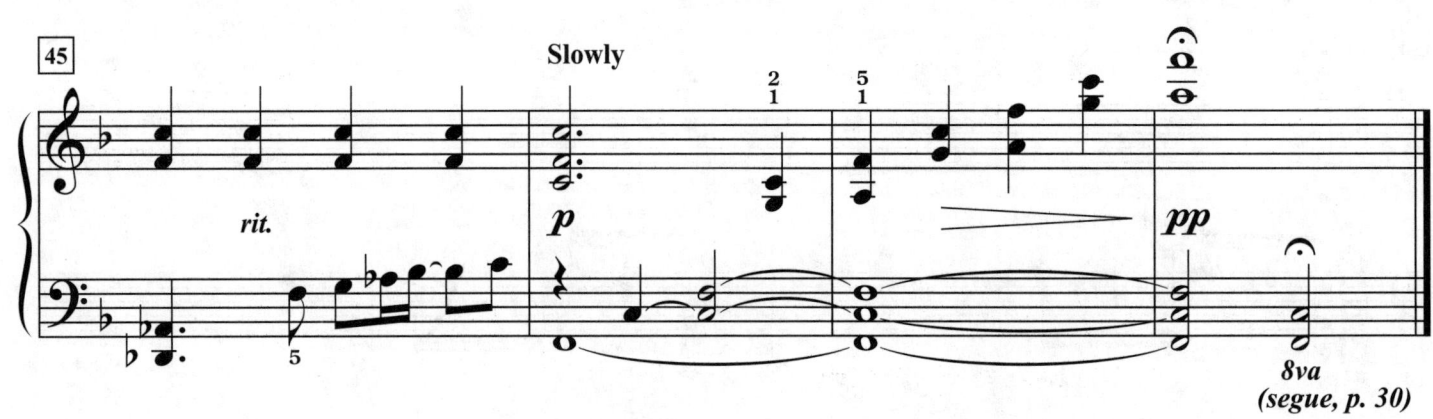

8va
(segue, p. 30)